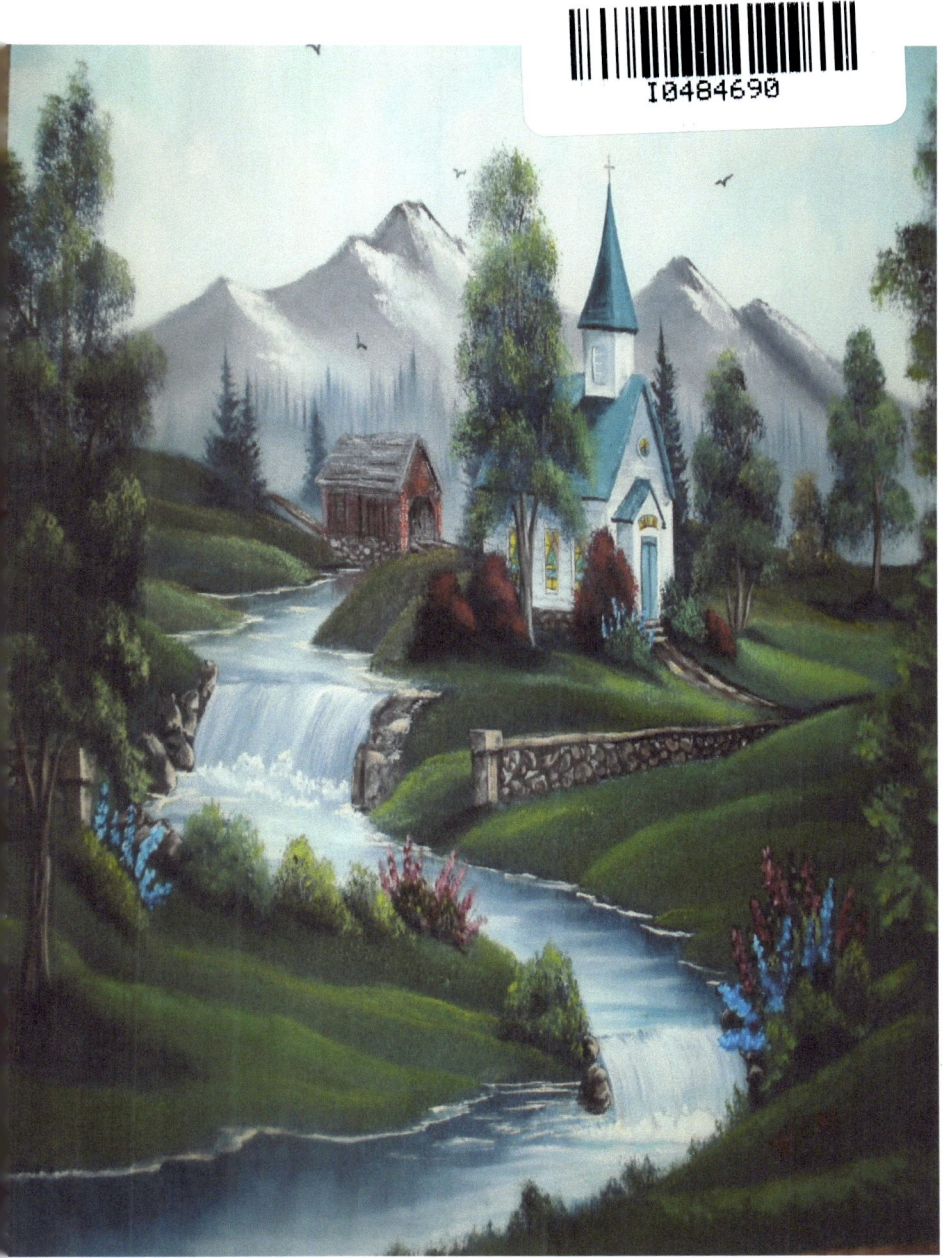

The Prettiest Psalm

The Art of Judith Webb

Other Books by Dirk Webb and Friends Publishing

A Warm Summer's Day
The Next Summer's Day
The Adventures of Mousey Carter McCloud

Www.dirkwebbandfriends.com

All scriptural passages—King James Version.

No part of this book can be copied, re-produced or transmitted in any form, in whole or in part with the exception of critical articles and reviews

Printed in the United States of America, 2011

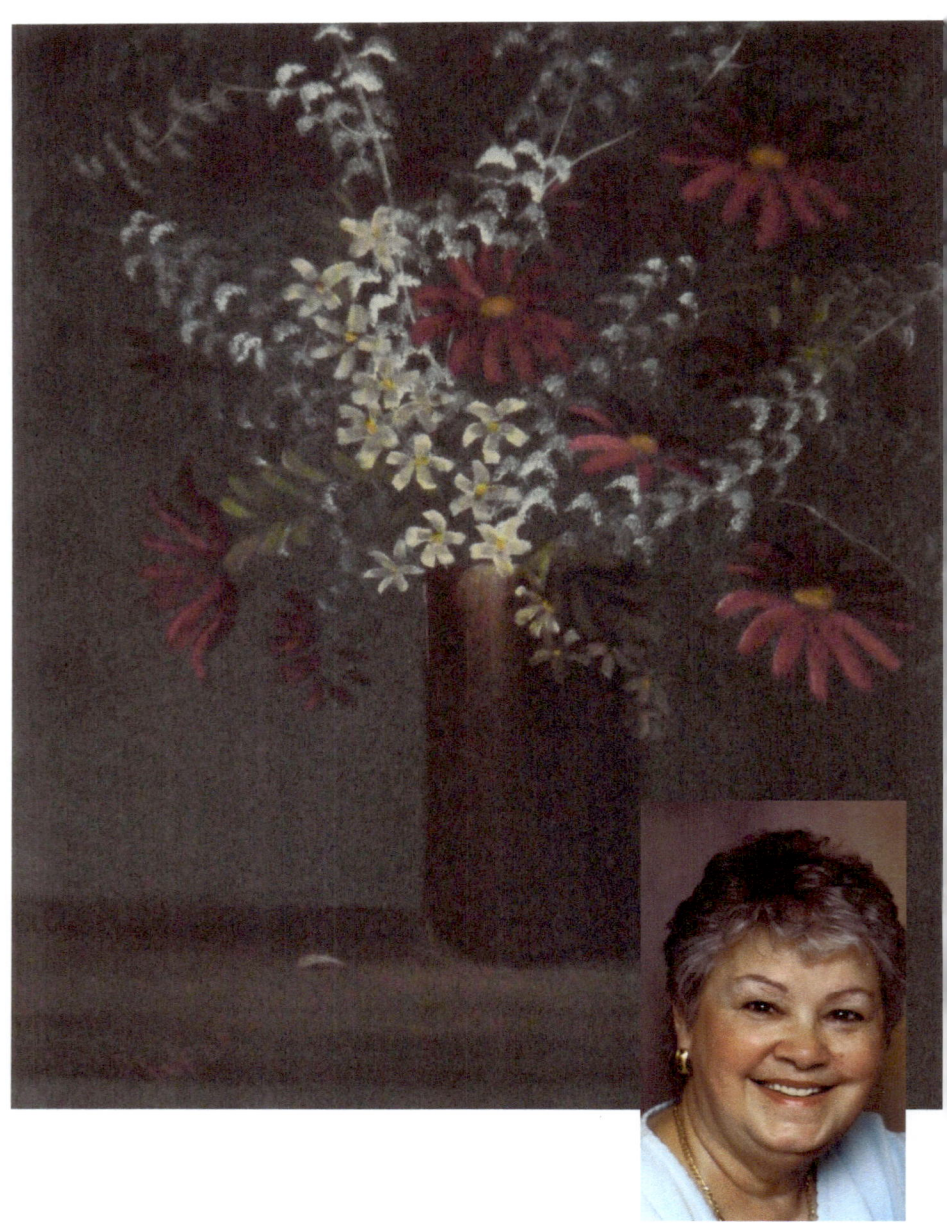

Psalm 105:1 says, "Bless the Lord, O my soul, and all that is within me, bless His holy name." We as believers sing, dance, write, preach and teach. There are so many ways to bless the Lord that there is no wonder the writer instructed us to use every means within our grasp or "all that is within me," to bless the Lord.

We were fortunate, as children, to enjoy watching our mother, Judith Webb, worship with the brush and canvas. From the time we were very small, we watched with wide eyes as she created beautiful, lush sceneries full of the creation of the God we love.

At the same time, we observed her, and our Dad worship the Lord with the reading of God's word. The Psalms always seemed to us the most beautiful and emotion-filled of the ancient writings as David and others poured out their hearts before God. So many believers, over the years, have comforted each other with the words of Psalm 23, "the Lord is my Shepherd…"

We are so proud to present two of our Mother's loves, her art and scripture, together in one collection: The Prettiest Psalm. We pray that you enjoy both the beauty of the words and the art.

Darla Webb Poore
Dirk Webb

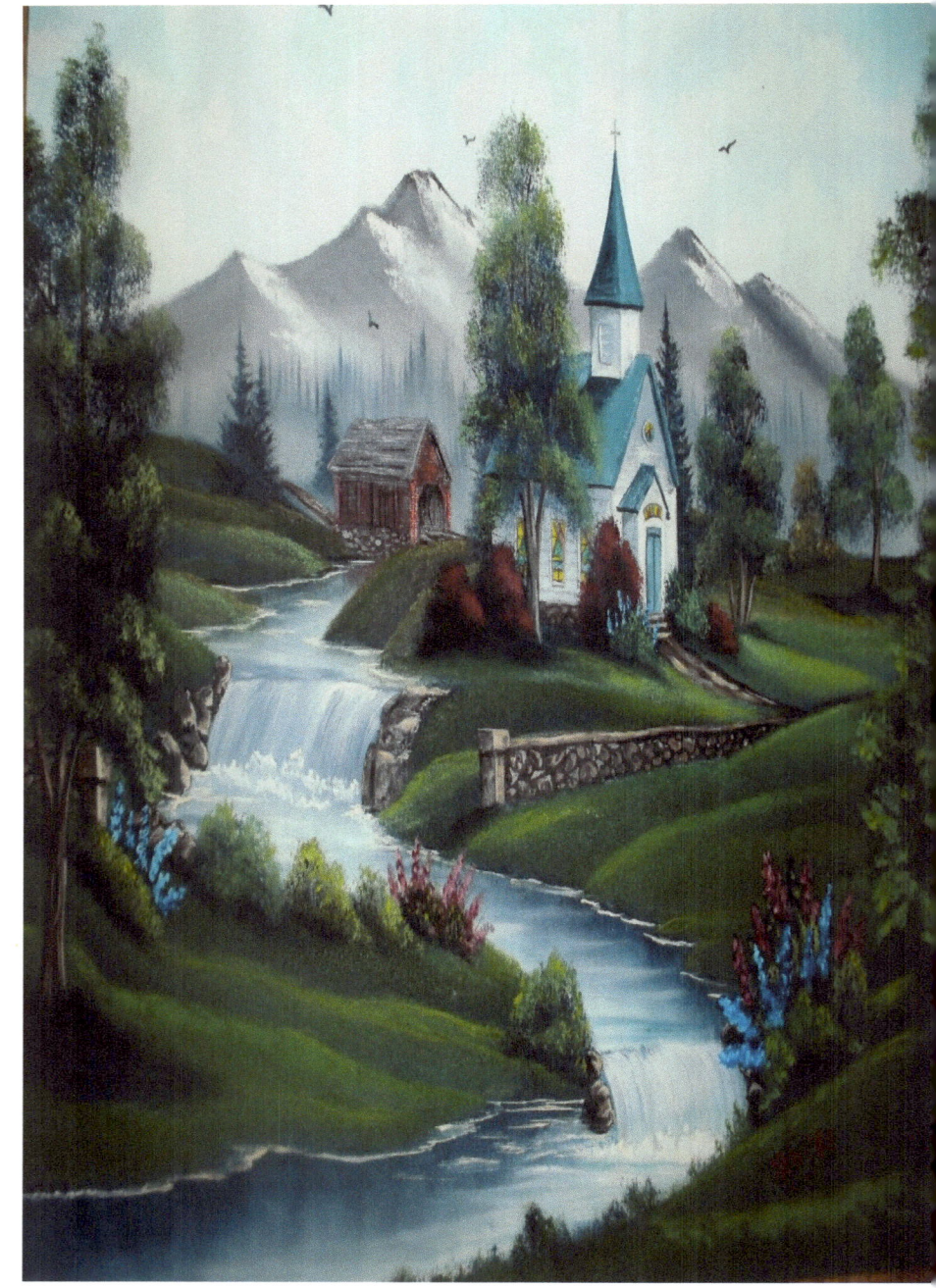

Psalm 1: 1-3

[1]Blessed is the man that walketh not in the counsel of the ungodly, nor standeth in the way of sinners, nor sitteth in the seat of the scornful.
[2]But his delight is in the law of the LORD; and in his law doth he meditate day and night.
[3]And he shall be like a tree planted by the rivers of water, that bringeth forth his fruit in his season; his leaf also shall not wither; and whatsoever he doeth shall prosper.

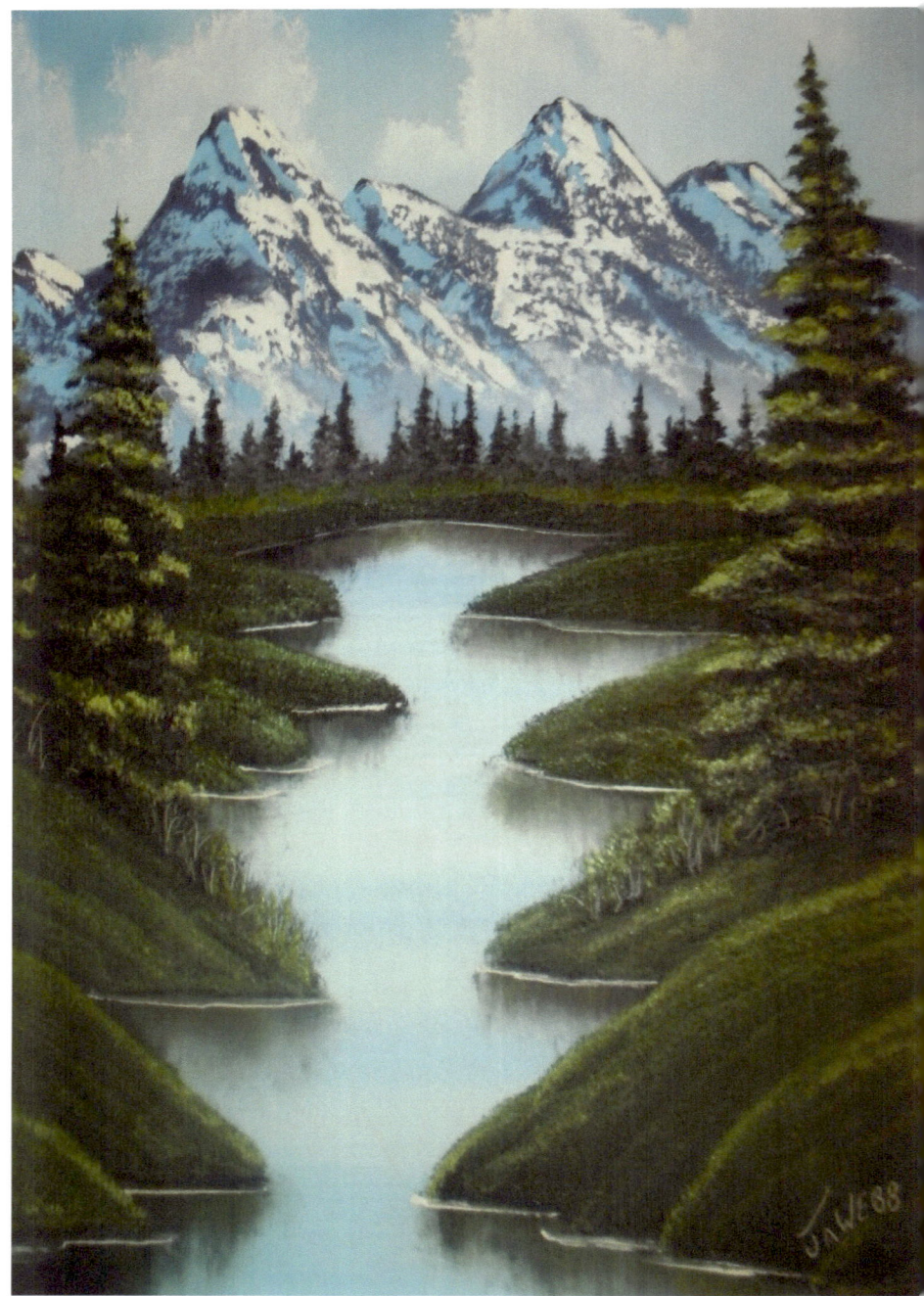

Psalm 8: 3-9

3When I consider thy heavens, the work of thy fingers, the moon and the stars, which thou hast ordained;
4What is man, that thou art mindful of him? and the son of man, that thou visitest him?
5For thou hast made him a little lower than the angels, and hast crowned him with glory and honour.
6Thou madest him to have dominion over the works of thy hands; thou hast put all things under his feet:
7All sheep and oxen, yea, and the beasts of the field;
8The fowl of the air, and the fish of the sea, and whatsoever passeth through the paths of the seas.
9O LORD our Lord, how excellent is thy name in all the earth!

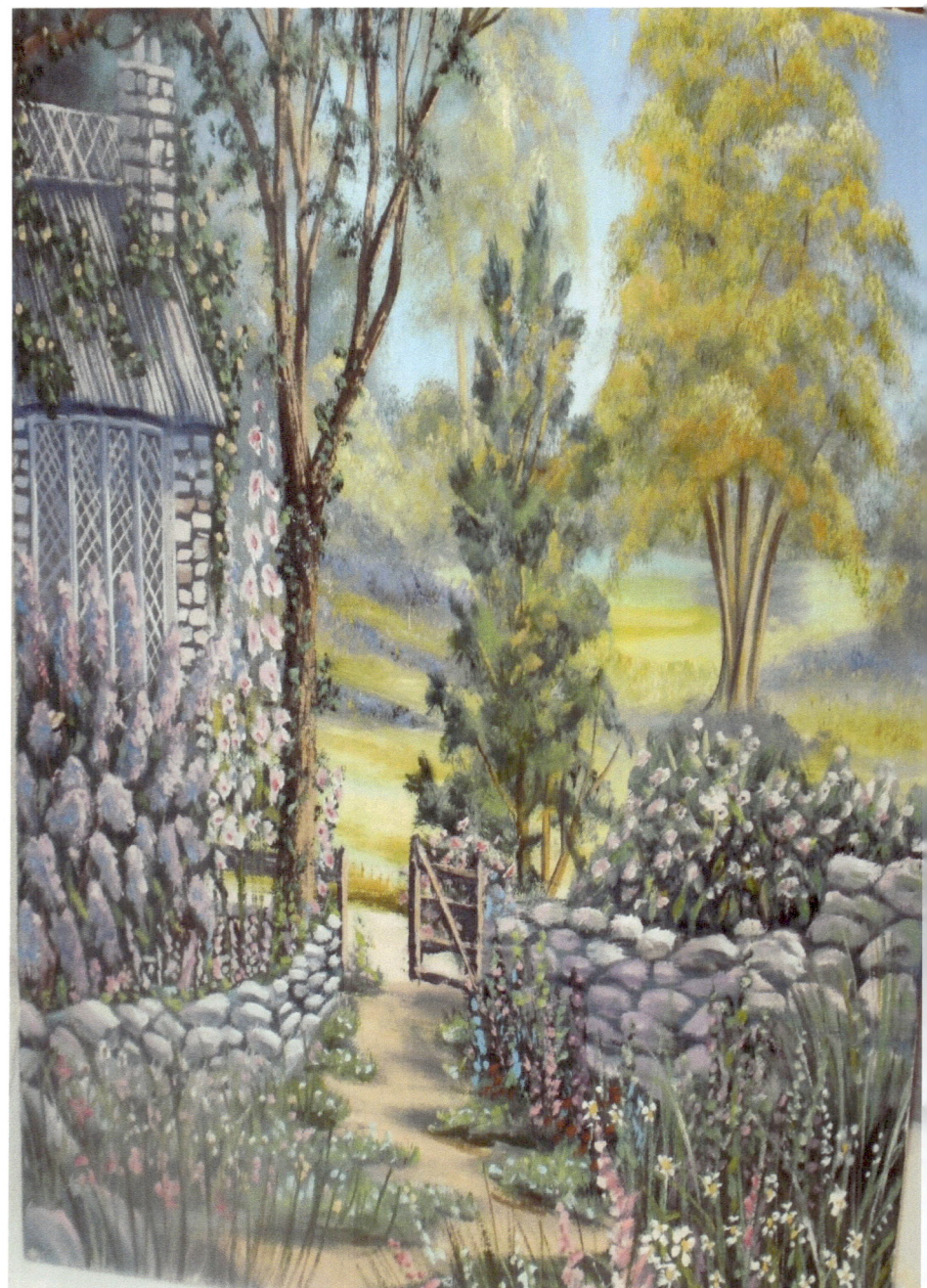

Psalm 23

1 The LORD is my shepherd; I shall not want.
2 He maketh me to lie down in green pastures: he leadeth me beside the still waters.
3 He restoreth my soul: he leadeth me in the paths of righteousness for his name's sake.
4 Yea, though I walk through the valley of the shadow of death, I will fear no evil: for thou art with me; thy rod and thy staff they comfort me.
5 Thou preparest a table before me in the presence of mine enemies: thou anointest my head with oil; my cup runneth over.
6 Surely goodness and mercy shall follow me all the days of my life: and I will dwell in the house of the LORD forever

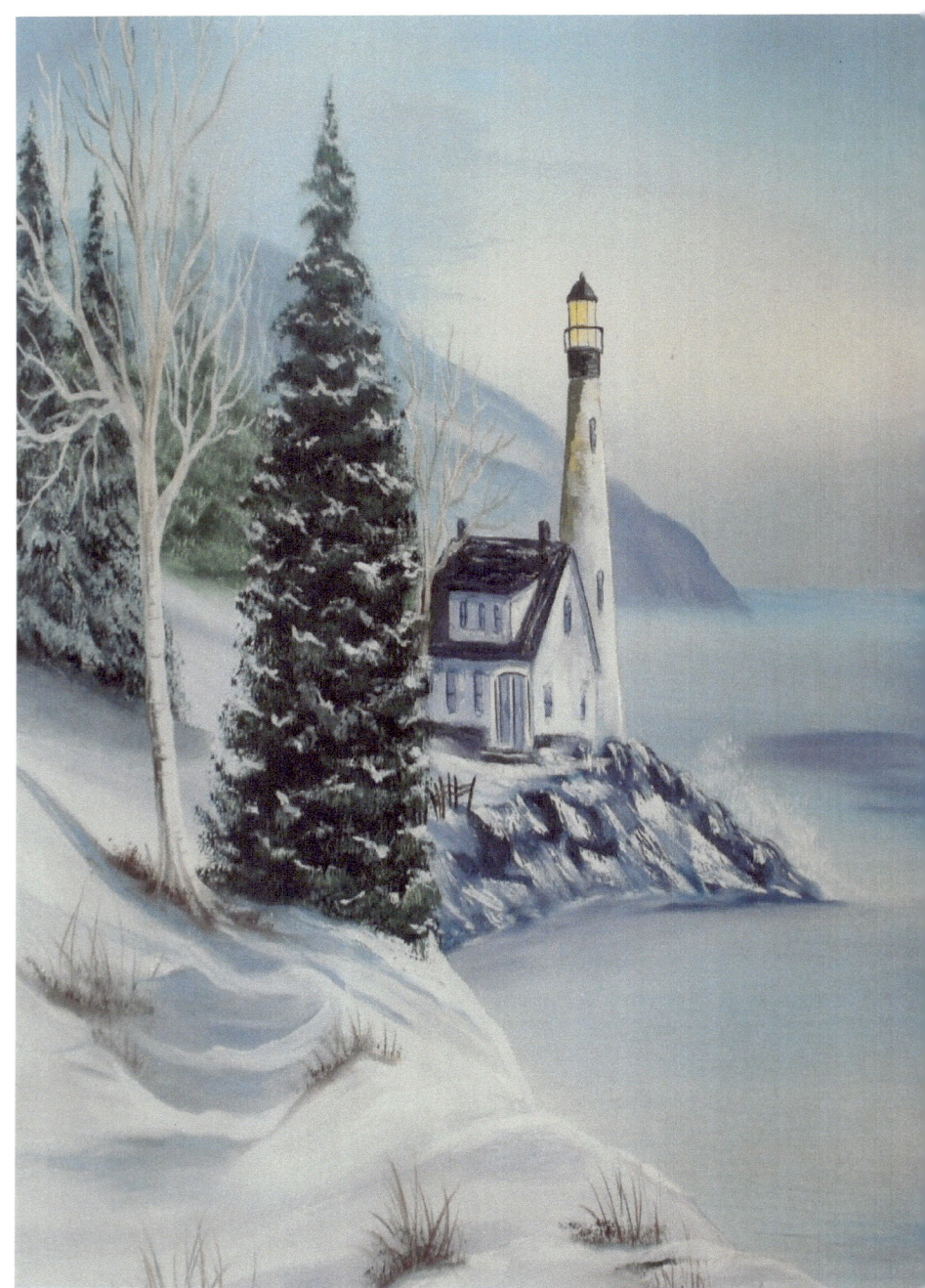

Psalm 24

¹The earth is the LORD's, and the fulness thereof; the world, and they that dwell therein.

²For he hath founded it upon the seas, and established it upon the floods.

³Who shall ascend into the hill of the LORD? or who shall stand in his holy place?

⁴He that hath clean hands, and a pure heart; who hath not lifted up his soul unto vanity, nor sworn deceitfully.

⁵He shall receive the blessing from the LORD, and righteousness from the God of his salvation.

⁶This is the generation of them that seek him, that seek thy face, O Jacob. Selah.

⁷Lift up your heads, O ye gates; and be ye lift up, ye everlasting doors; and the King of glory shall come in.

⁸Who is this King of glory? The LORD strong and mighty, the LORD mighty in battle.

⁹Lift up your heads, O ye gates; even lift them up, ye everlasting doors; and the King of glory shall come in.

¹⁰Who is this King of glory? The LORD of hosts, he is the King of glory. Selah.

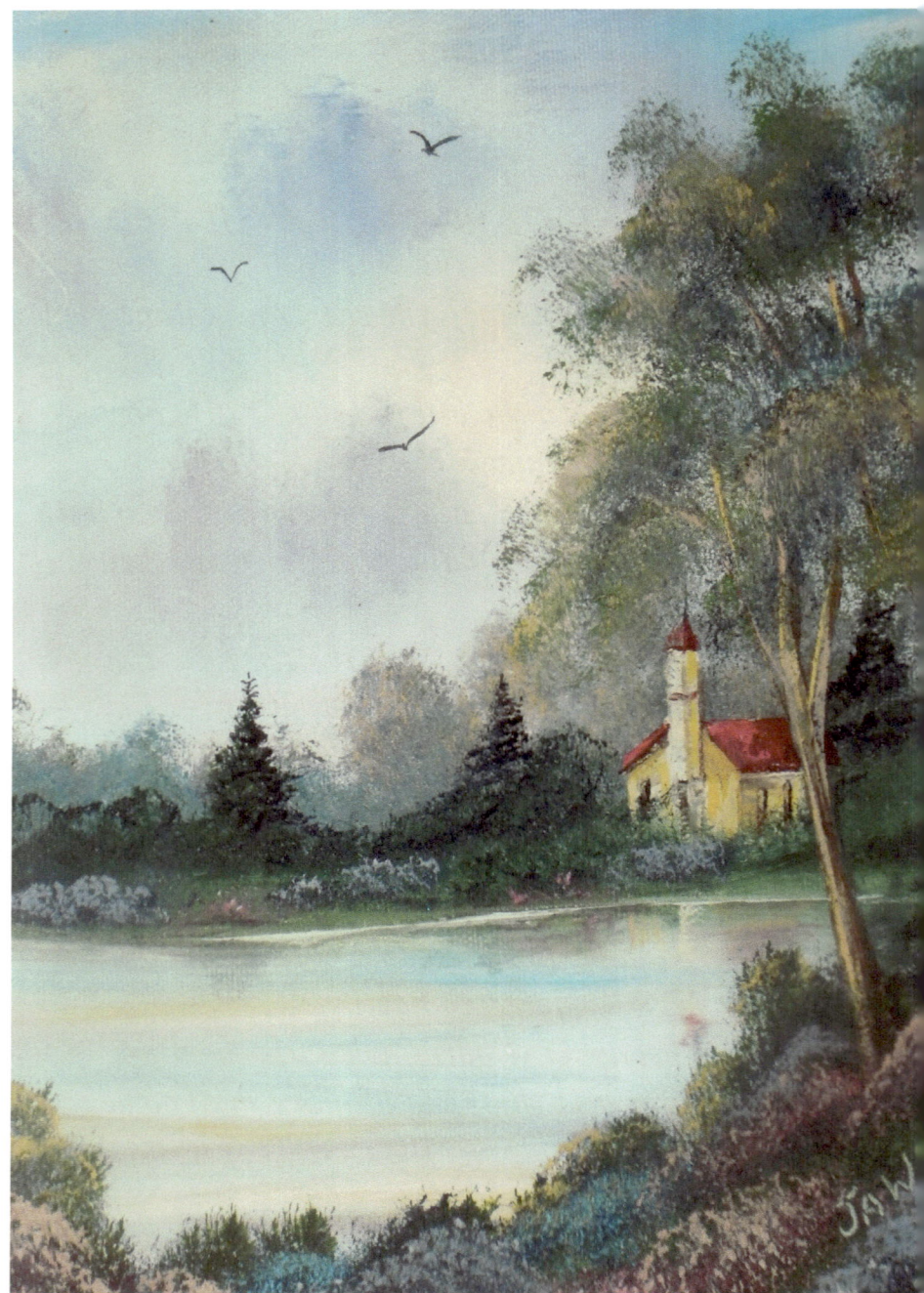

16

Psalm 25: 4-6

⁴Shew me thy ways, O LORD; teach me thy paths.
⁵Lead me in thy truth, and teach me: for thou art the God of my salvation; on thee do I wait all the day.
⁶Remember, O LORD, thy tender mercies and thy lovingkindnesses; for they have been ever of old.

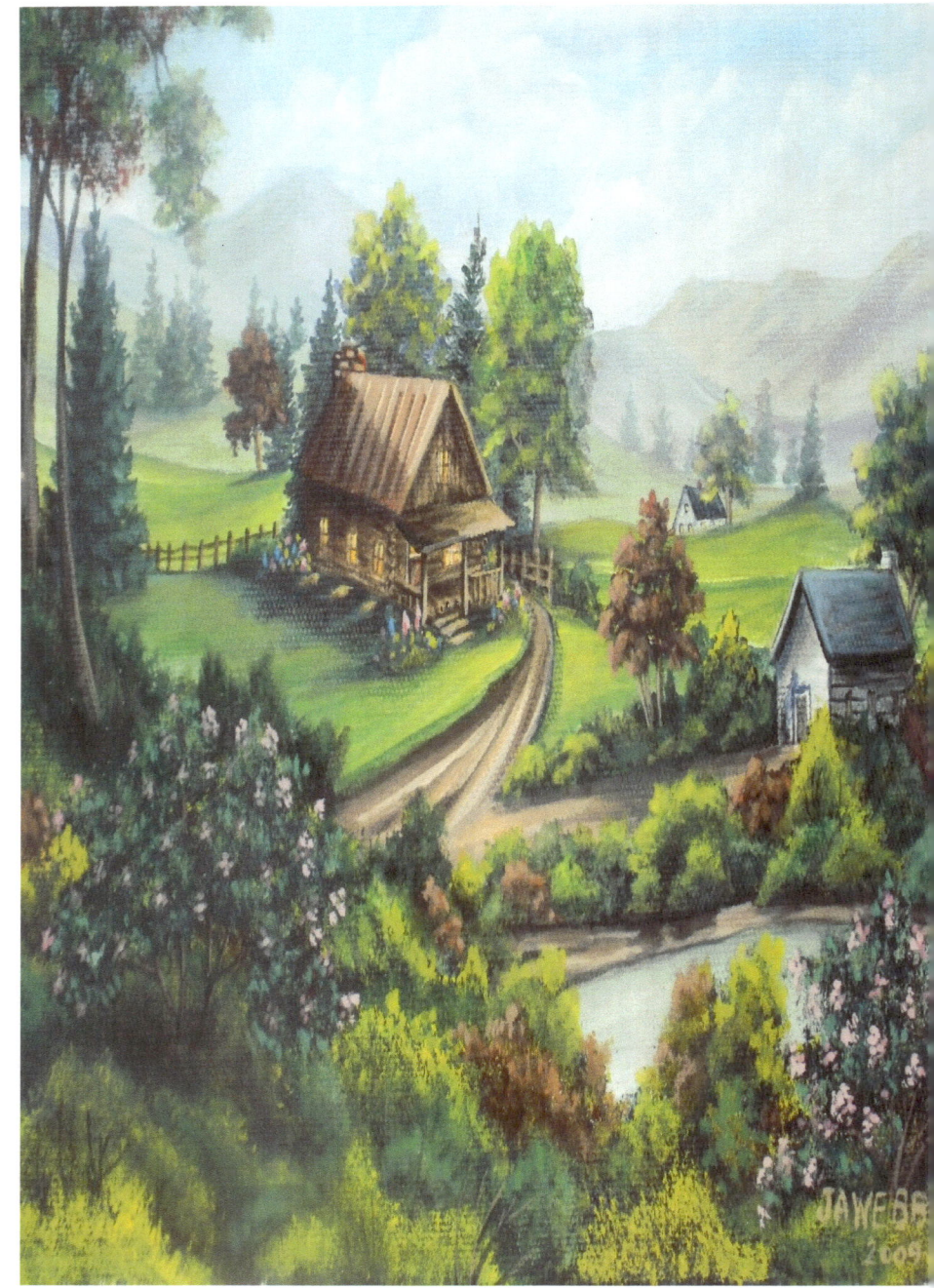

Psalm 57: 7-11

7 My heart is fixed, O God, my heart is fixed: I will sing and give praise.

8 Awake up, my glory; awake, psaltery and harp: I myself will awake early.

9 I will praise thee, O Lord, among the people: I will sing unto thee among the nations.

10 For thy mercy is great unto the heavens, and thy truth unto the clouds.

11 Be thou exalted, O God, above the heavens: let thy glory be above all the earth.

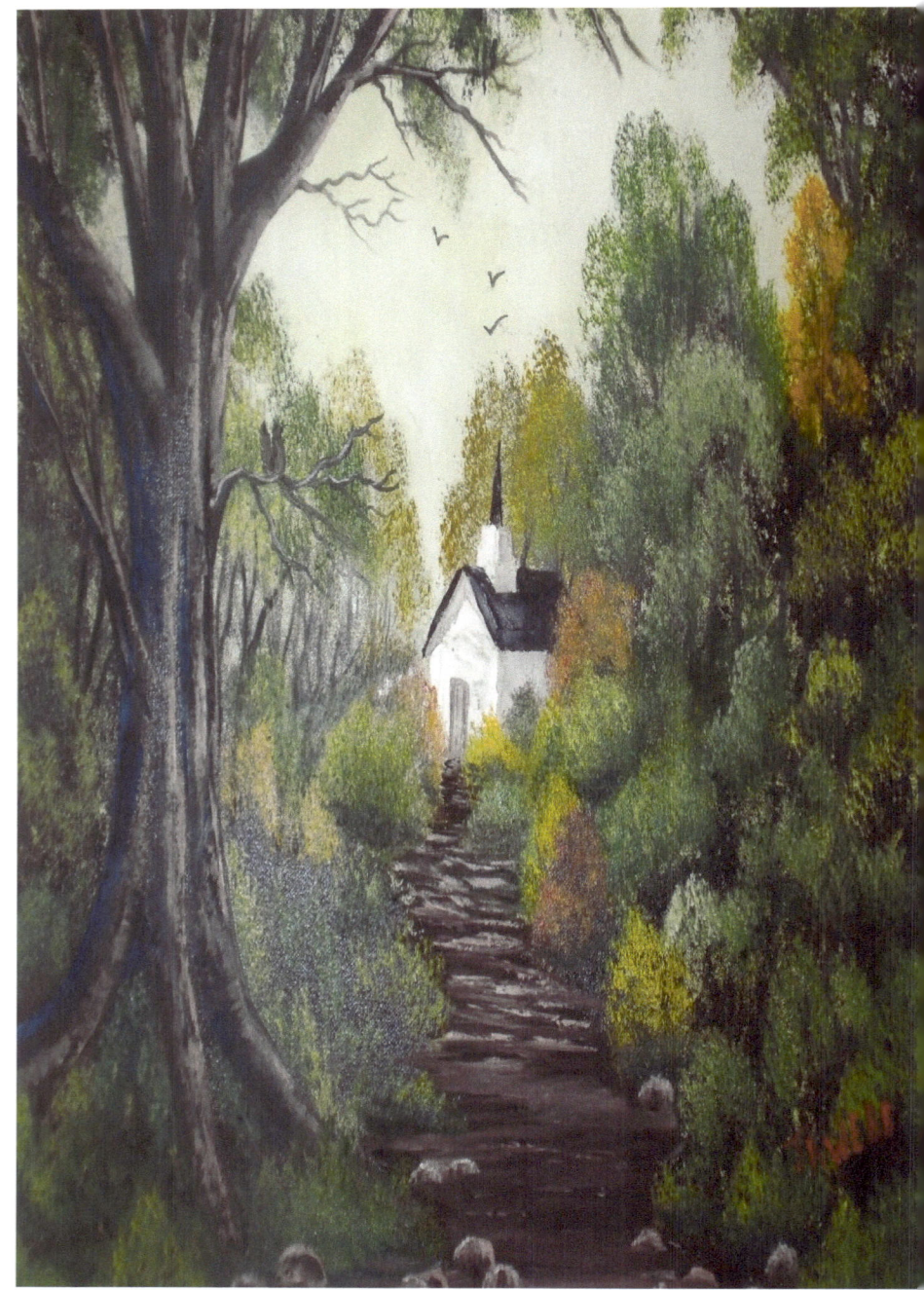

Psalm 65: 9-13

⁹*Thou visitest the earth, and waterest it: thou greatly enrichest it with the river of God, which is full of water: thou preparest them corn, when thou hast so provided for it.*

¹⁰*Thou waterest the ridges thereof abundantly: thou settlest the furrows thereof: thou makest it soft with showers: thou blessest the springing thereof.*

¹¹*Thou crownest the year with thy goodness; and thy paths drop fatness.*

¹²*They drop upon the pastures of the wilderness: and the little hills rejoice on every side.*

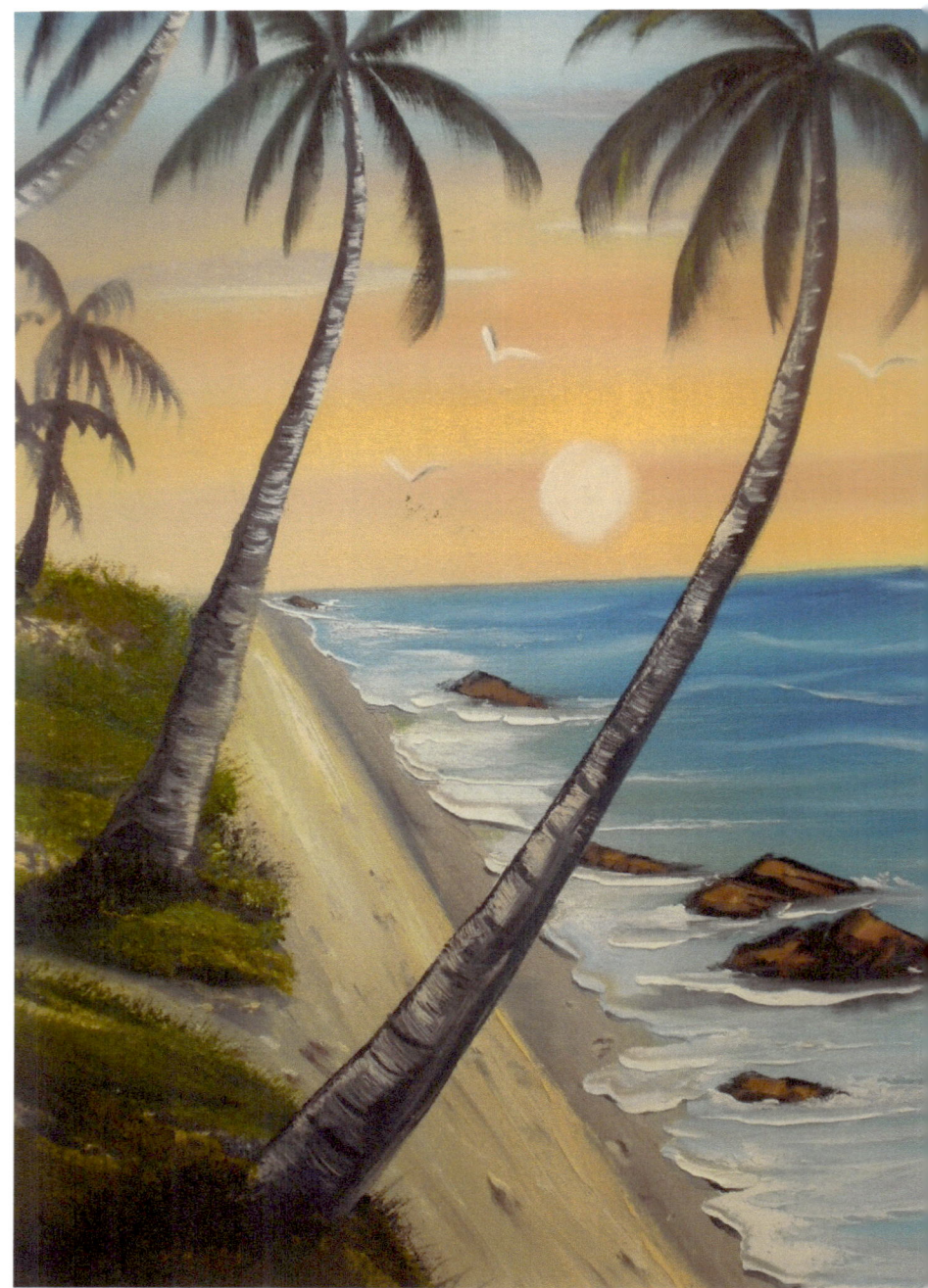

Psalm 91

[1]He that dwelleth in the secret place of the most High shall abide under the shadow of the Almighty.

[2]I will say of the LORD, He is my refuge and my fortress: my God; in him will I trust.

[3]Surely he shall deliver thee from the snare of the fowler, and from the noisome pestilence.

[4]He shall cover thee with his feathers, and under his wings shalt thou trust: his truth shall be thy shield and buckler.

[5]Thou shalt not be afraid for the terror by night; nor for the arrow that flieth by day;

[6]Nor for the pestilence that walketh in darkness; nor for the destruction that wasteth at noonday.

[7]A thousand shall fall at thy side, and ten thousand at thy right hand; but it shall not come nigh thee.

[8]Only with thine eyes shalt thou behold and see the reward of the wicked.

[9]Because thou hast made the LORD, which is my refuge, even the most High, thy habitation;

[10]There shall no evil befall thee, neither shall any plague come nigh thy dwelling.

[11]For he shall give his angels charge over thee, to keep thee in all thy ways.

[12]They shall bear thee up in their hands, lest thou dash thy foot against a stone.

[13]Thou shalt tread upon the lion and adder: the young lion and the dragon shalt thou trample under feet.

[14]Because he hath set his love upon me, therefore will I deliver him: I will set him on high, because he hath known my name.

[15]He shall call upon me, and I will answer him: I will be with him in trouble; I will deliver him, and honour him.

[16]With long life will I satisfy him, and shew him my salvation.

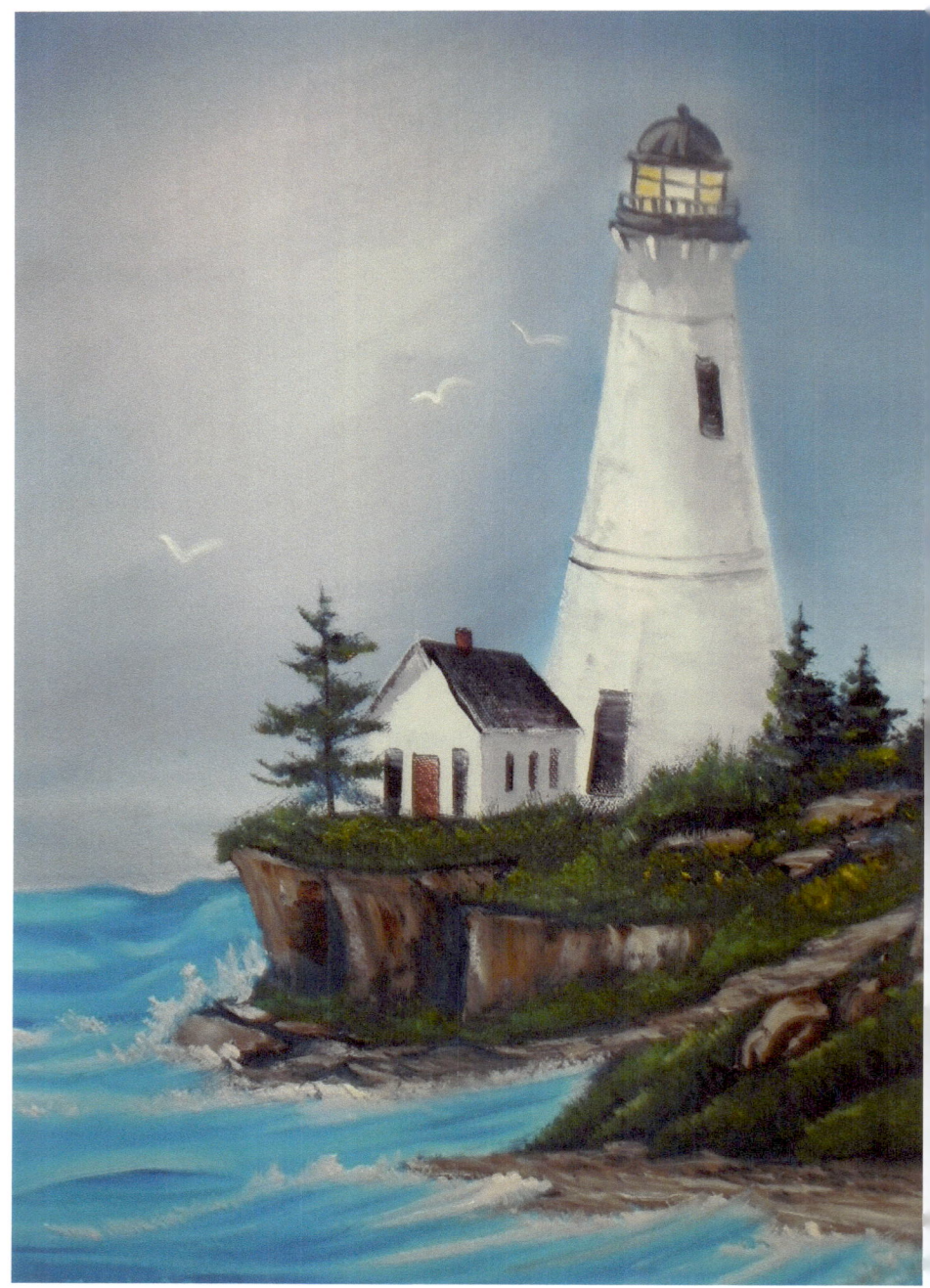

Psalm 95: 1-7

¹O come, let us sing unto the LORD: let us make a joyful noise to the rock of our salvation.

²Let us come before his presence with thanksgiving, and make a joyful noise unto him with psalms.

³For the LORD is a great God, and a great King above all gods.

⁴In his hand are the deep places of the earth: the strength of the hills is his also.

⁵The sea is his, and he made it: and his hands formed the dry land.

⁶O come, let us worship and bow down: let us kneel before the LORD our maker.

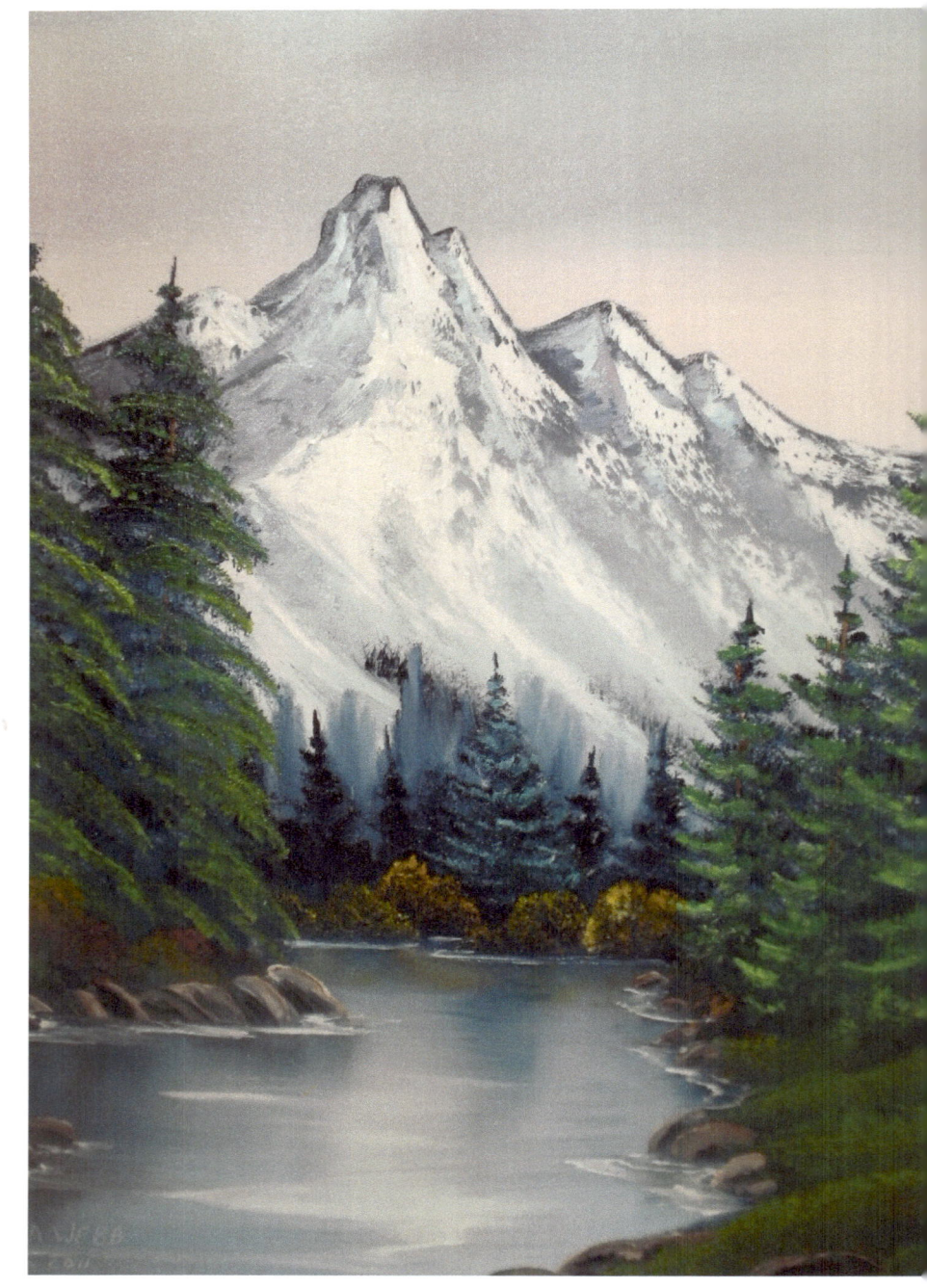

Psalm 100

¹Make a joyful noise unto the LORD, all ye lands.
²Serve the LORD with gladness: come before his presence with singing.
³Know ye that the LORD he is God: it is he that hath made us, and not we ourselves; we are his people, and the sheep of his pasture.
⁴Enter into his gates with thanksgiving, and into his courts with praise: be thankful unto him, and bless his name.

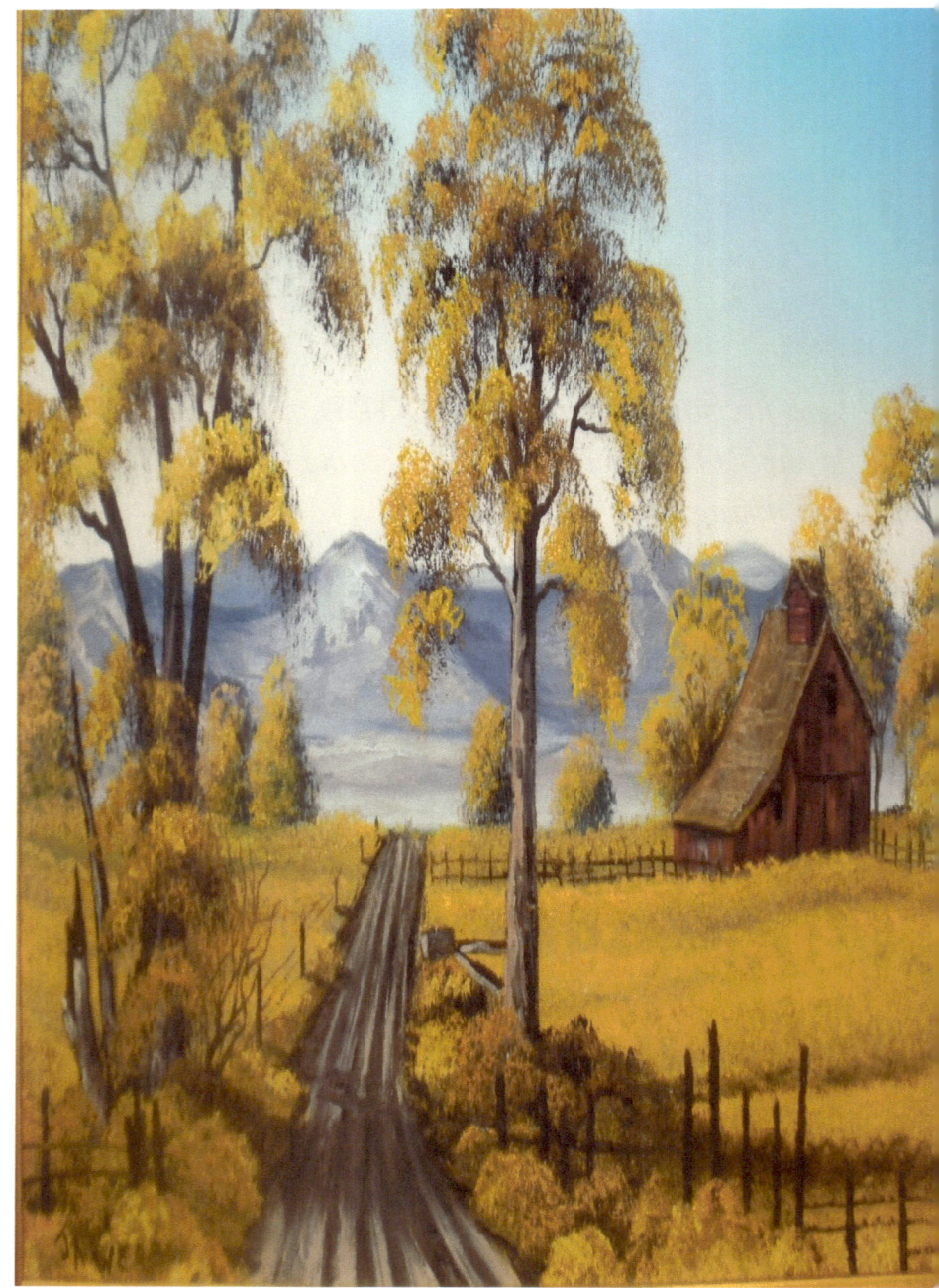

28

Psalm 103

¹Bless the LORD, O my soul: and all that is within me, bless his holy name.

²Bless the LORD, O my soul, and forget not all his benefits:

³Who forgiveth all thine iniquities; who healeth all thy diseases;

⁴Who redeemeth thy life from destruction; who crowneth thee with lovingkindness and tender mercies;

⁵Who satisfieth thy mouth with good things; so that thy youth is renewed like the eagle's.

⁶The LORD executeth righteousness and judgment for all that are oppressed.

⁷He made known his ways unto Moses, his acts unto the children of Israel.

⁸The LORD is merciful and gracious, slow to anger, and plenteous in mercy.

⁹He will not always chide: neither will he keep his anger for ever.

¹⁰He hath not dealt with us after our sins; nor rewarded us according to our iniquities.

¹¹For as the heaven is high above the earth, so great is his mercy toward them that fear him.

¹²As far as the east is from the west, so far hath he removed our transgressions from us.

¹³Like as a father pitieth his children, so the LORD pitieth them that fear him.

¹⁴For he knoweth our frame; he remembereth that we are dust.

¹⁵As for man, his days are as grass: as a flower of the field, so he flourisheth.

¹⁶For the wind passeth over it, and it is gone; and the place thereof shall know it no more.

¹⁷But the mercy of the LORD is from everlasting to everlasting upon them that fear him, and his righteousness unto children's children;

¹⁸To such as keep his covenant, and to those that remember his commandments to do them.

¹⁹The LORD hath prepared his throne in the heavens; and his kingdom ruleth over all.

²⁰Bless the LORD, ye his angels, that excel in strength, that do his commandments, hearkening unto the voice of his word.

²¹Bless ye the LORD, all ye his hosts; ye ministers of his, that do his pleasure.

²²Bless the LORD, all his works in all places of his dominion: bless the LORD, O my soul.

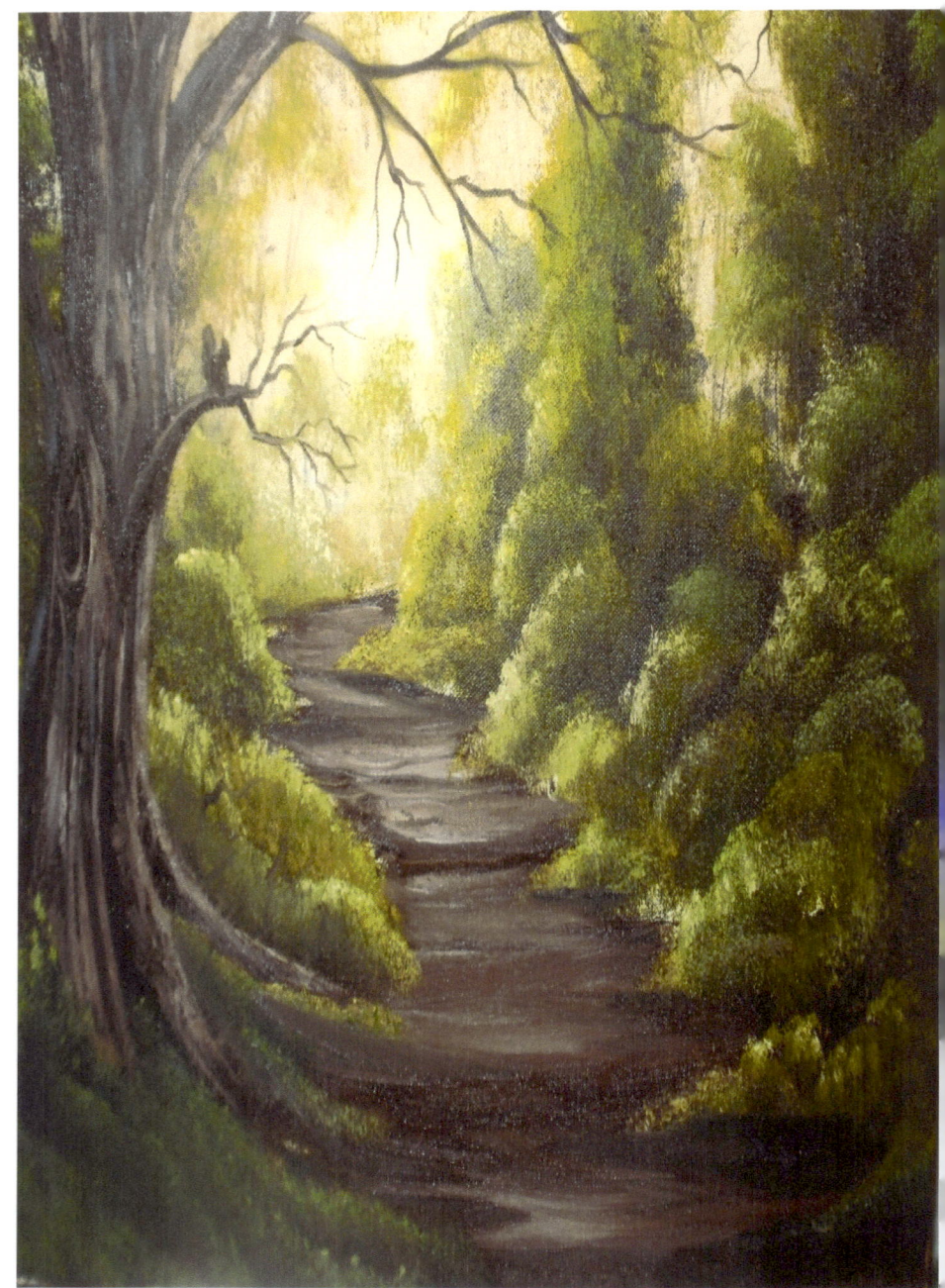

Psalm 145: 1-5

[1] I will extol thee, my God, O king; and I will bless thy name for ever and ever.
[2] Every day will I bless thee; and I will praise thy name for ever and ever.
[3] Great is the LORD, and greatly to be praised; and his greatness is unsearchable.
[4] One generation shall praise thy works to another, and shall declare thy mighty acts.
[5] I will speak of the glorious honour of thy majesty, and of thy wondrous works.

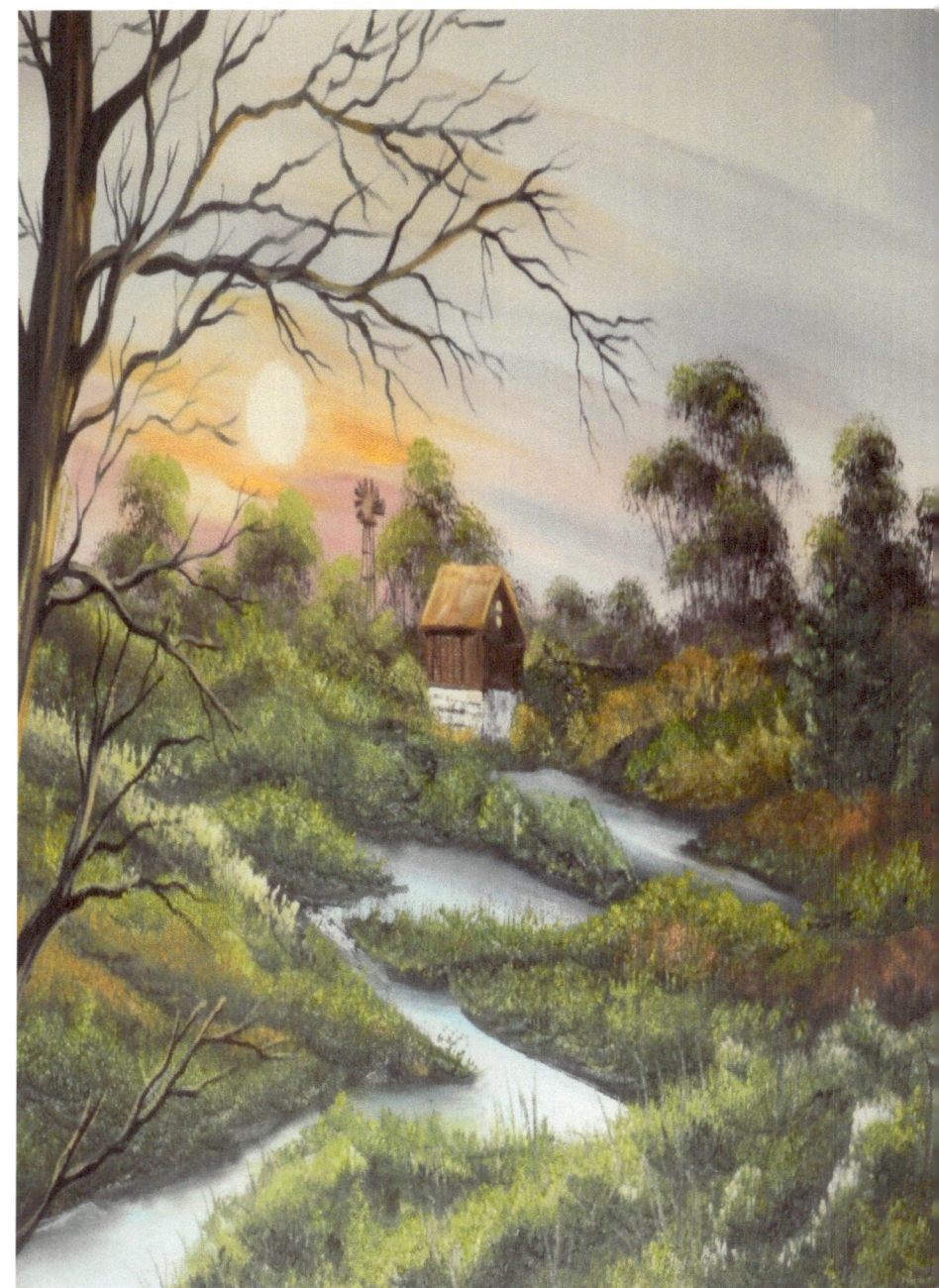

Psalm 113: 1-5

1Praise ye the LORD. Praise, O ye servants of the LORD, praise the name of the LORD.
2Blessed be the name of the LORD from this time forth and for evermore.
3From the rising of the sun unto the going down of the same the LORD's name is to be praised.
4The LORD is high above all nations, and his glory above the heavens.
5Who is like unto the LORD our God, who dwelleth on high.

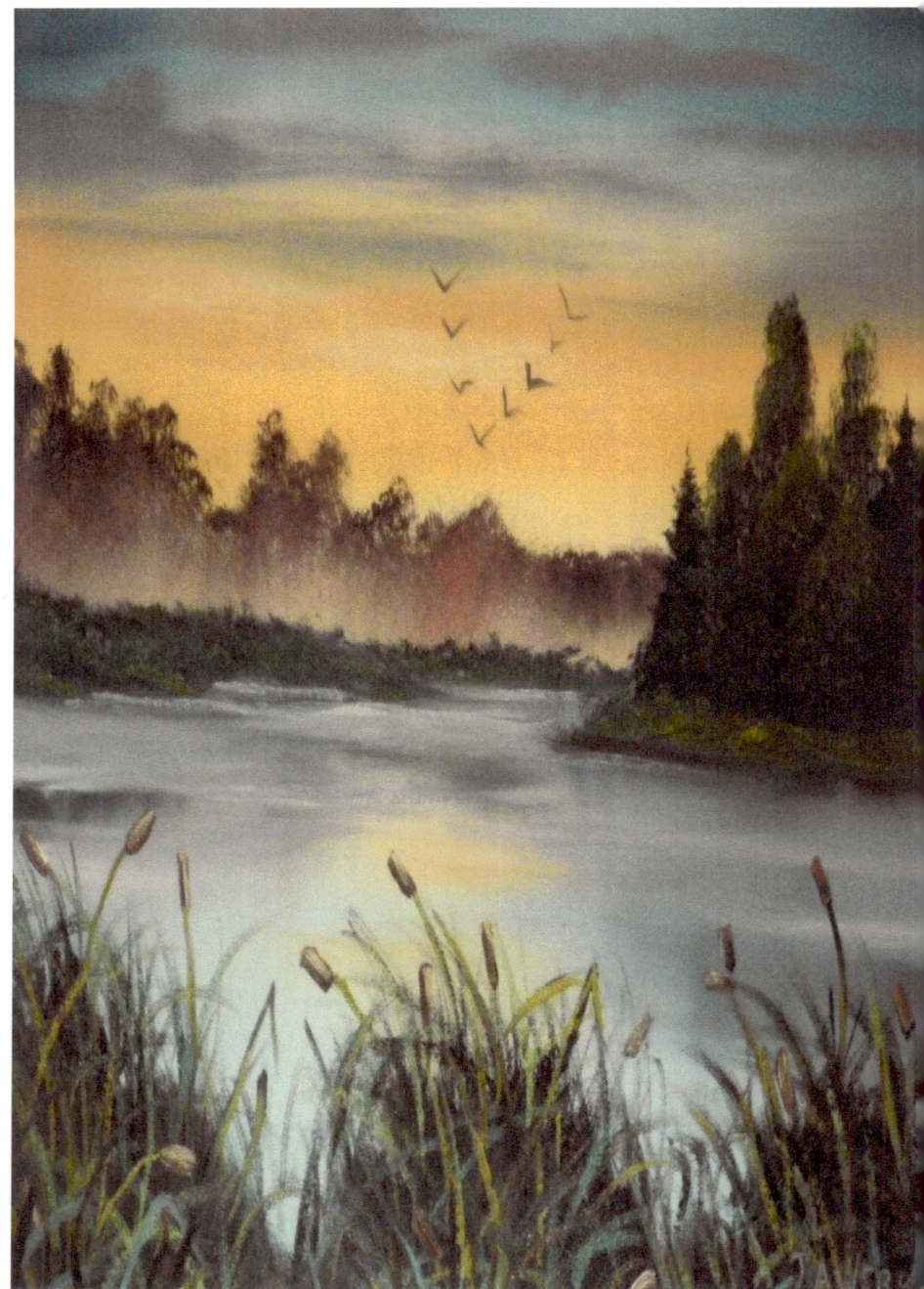

Psalm 108: 3-5

³ I will praise thee, O LORD, among the people: and I will sing praises unto thee among the nations.
⁴ For thy mercy is great above the heavens: and thy truth reacheth unto the clouds.
⁵ Be thou exalted, O God, above the heavens: and thy glory above all the earth.

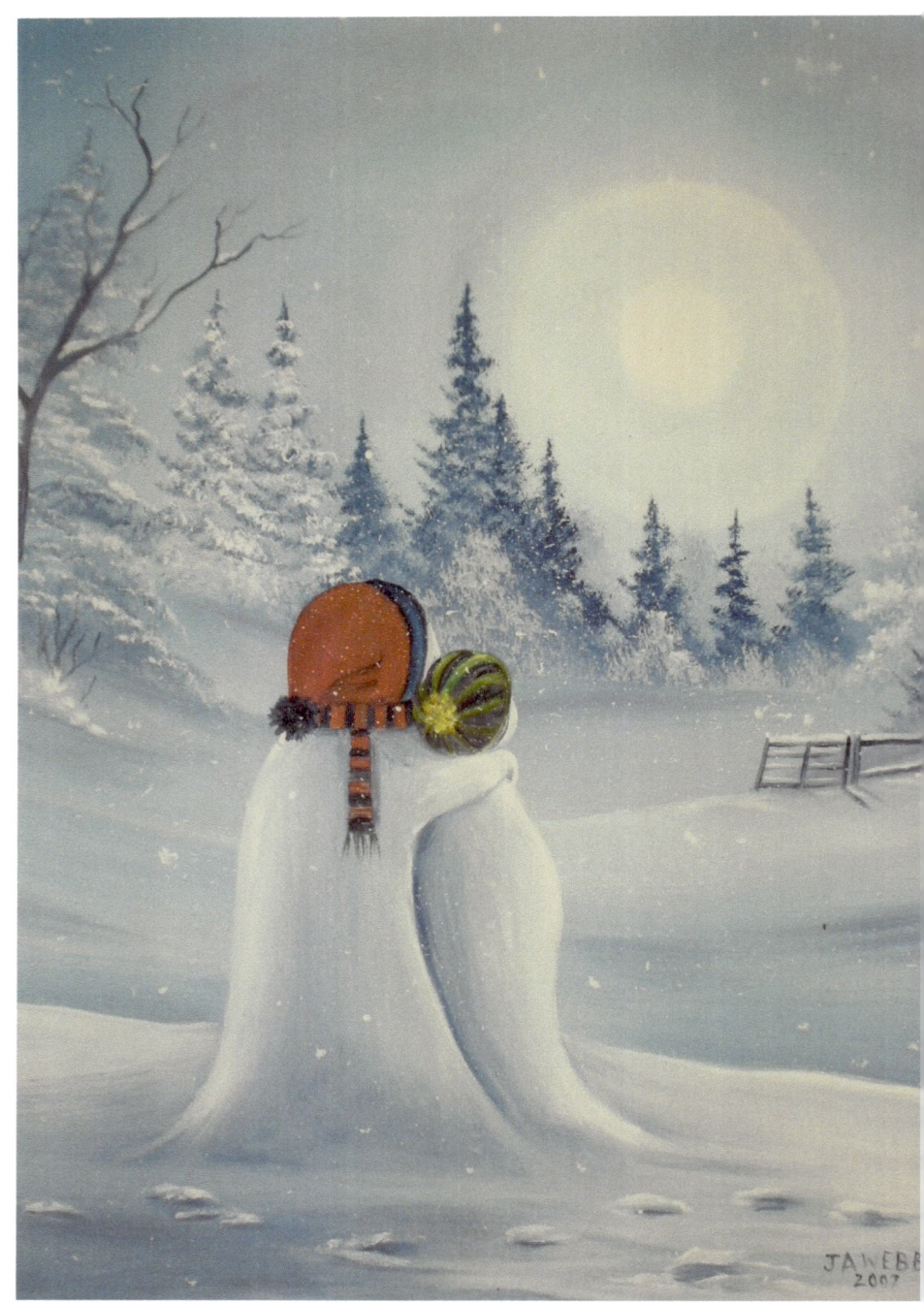

Psalm 139: 1-10

1O lord, thou hast searched me, and known me.
2Thou knowest my downsitting and mine uprising, thou understandest my thought afar off.
3Thou compassest my path and my lying down, and art acquainted with all my ways.
4For there is not a word in my tongue, but, lo, O LORD, thou knowest it altogether.
5Thou hast beset me behind and before, and laid thine hand upon me.
6Such knowledge is too wonderful for me; it is high, I cannot attain unto it.
7Whither shall I go from thy spirit? or whither shall I flee from thy presence?
8If I ascend up into heaven, thou art there: if I make my bed in hell, behold, thou art there.
9If I take the wings of the morning, and dwell in the uttermost parts of the sea;
10Even there shall thy hand lead me, and thy right hand shall hold me.

www.ingramcontent.com/pod-product-compliance
Lightning Source LLC
Chambersburg PA
CBHW041147180526
45159CB00002BB/747